WireGrassroots Marketing

By
Marcie Harris Nye

WireGrassroots Marketing

Acknowledgements

I'd like to thank my family for their patience, support and encouragement; especially my husband, Dr. Laurence W. Kuhn, who not only stood by me as I worked out how to write a book that wasn't an academic treatise, but even went so far as to redecorate my office to make it more work friendly.

I also want to thank the business owners who allowed me to write about their marketing, and their many contributions to tweak the book, provide photos, and in some cases, just plain encouragement when I felt stuck: Hope Johnson of Friend Bank, Jimmy Rane of Great Southern Wood Preserving and Huggin' Molly's, Jeremy Pate of Folklore Brewery and Meadery, Earnie Faulk of Earnie's Snowballs and Chili Dogs, Brittany Hurst Jolly of Hurst's Wiregrass Taekwondo Center, and J.D. Sadler of Ravenwood. You folks inspired me to write about grassroots marketing because you do it so well. I appreciate your marketing, as well as your help in my book project.

Table of Contents

Introduction

Grassroots marketing, often called guerilla marketing, is defined as marketing from the ground up—starting with small groups who expand your marketing message to larger groups. It is often unconventional, nontraditional and lower in cost than more common methods of marketing.

In today's connected world, where we are *constantly* being bombarded by marketing, a lot of the messages are not heard. It has been said that we are exposed to 10,000 marketing messages every day. Is it any wonder that the modern consumer shuts out all but a few of these messages?

So, how can you cut through the clutter of marketing so that *your* message is heard? Well, you have to capture the attention of your target audience, and you have to do it in a way that doesn't trigger their alarm bells that you are trying to sell them something.

That's why I **absolutely love** grassroots marketing. It is interesting, creative, and it can be fun! Best of all, it is comparatively low cost and can provide a much greater return on investment (ROI) than traditional marketing.

The best grassroots marketers use multiple techniques that spread across various projects, and then dovetail together in order to create a wide reaching presence. The programs are complicated and detailed. In combination, they are irresistible, yet subtle in their ability to influence the consumer. And when all the elements are in place, it is almost magical—hypnotic in its appeal.

As I look around the area, I can see how a few local businesses are using grassroots marketing. Some are doing it on their own, others hire a professional marketing company. Perhaps this book will stimulate you to start thinking about marketing in a different way-- one that is more effective, and that can often be done better on a local level.

Yella Fella and Huggin' Molly's

My absolute favorite grassroots marketing can be seen on Highway 431, south of Abbeville. You've probably seen it yourself and gotten a chuckle out of it. It's a dilapidated old barn…falling apart, rotting out, being slowly absorbed back into the earth. Stretched across the side that faces the highway is a huge yellow banner that reads, "SHOULD'VE USED YELLAWOOD". I crack up every time I see it. I don't have any idea what the ROI for that banner is, but it cuts through the clutter, makes me laugh, and creates affinity for the product. It is brilliant, as are a lot of Jimmy Rane's promotions. He's the head of Great Southern Wood Preserving, which makes the YellaWood brand of lumber, and he also operates Huggin' Molly's restaurant.

I also love that the way Mr. Rane has created a destination experience in the historic downtown area of Abbeville.

The antiques in the shop windows are really interesting and the overall effect is that you have stepped back in time. Dead center of that historic shopping area is Huggin' Molly's. The old fashioned soda shop atmosphere has recreated that simple, bygone era. From the black and white tile, and the beautiful wood and antiques, to the gun from the movie "Old Yeller" …the theme is both interesting and it is engaging. The Huggin' Molly ghost story is delightful. And, don't forget the "Home of Huggin' Molly's" sign at the Abbeville city limits. *Wow!*

These things get you in the door of Huggin' Molly's, but the quality of the food and the refreshingly great service keep you coming back.

Mr. Rane has further used grassroots marketing by

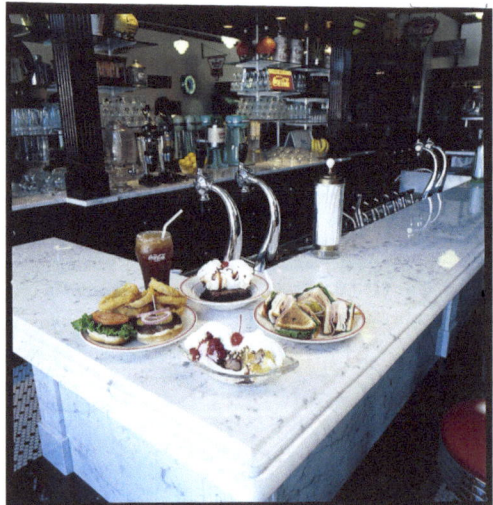

selling antique style postcards at the cashier's counter. I've sent out dozens of them, and often when out of town guests come to visit, they want to go to Huggin' Molly's and experience for themselves the soda shop that time forgot. Mr. Rane has gotten *me* to do his marketing for him, and he has gotten *me* to pay for it! I *bought* the postcards. I *paid* for the mailing. I *sent* the postcards to my network. *And* I took my friends and family to his establishment. The whole thing is just beautiful from a marketing standpoint.

The final piece of the grassroots marketing strategy at Huggin' Molly's is the staff. They *can* greet every customer as they come in the door *with a smile*. They *can* be upbeat and courteous. They *can* provide great tasting food quickly. They *can* deliver that food to you with a positive attitude. They *can* keep the place clean. They *can* leave their personal problems at home. They *can* thank you for your business. Everything else would be wasted if the staff could not meet, *and exceed* expectations for quality of product and noteworthy service. That, in and of itself, is marketing, because it compels customers to talk about the place, and to recommend it to people they know.

How <u>You</u> Can Use It

Right about now, you might be thinking, "That's all well and good, but my business is different. What does this have to do with me? I'm a plumber (or whatever), and I don't see how the marketing of treated lumber or a restaurant means anything to my business." The truth of the matter is, that on some level certain things pertain to every business. You can't have a business without having customers. You can't *stay* in business, if you can't *keep* customers.

Let's look a little deeper at how Mr. Rane's marketing works. In the first bullet point on page 11, we see that his organizations have **excellent customer service**. Customer service is sort of like the weather—everybody talks about it, but nobody seems to do anything about it. We all agree that it is important, yet too often what we actually get is grossly inadequate.

A trip to Huggin' Molly's will help you to define exactly what customer service is. From the first greeting as you walk in the door, to the friendly smiling faces of the wait staff, the quality and quantity of the food, the attentiveness of the servers, and the speed of getting your check and paying; it all comes together into one outstanding experience. And that, I think, is the essence of what we keep hearing from business and marketing consultants, *"It's the Customer Experience"*. If a client walks away from an exchange with you feeling uplifted, energized, or impressed, you have succeeded. There are some things in life where good enough is good enough, but customer service is *not* one of those things.

All the marketing in the world won't help you if your customer service doesn't meet **and exceed** your clients' expectations. Bringing in more customers who are disappointed with their experience will only speed up the demise of your enterprise. On the other hand, in today's climate, it is actually pretty easy to be exceptional at customer service.

Exceptional customer service does something else for you that you can't get any other way; it gets people talking about you in a positive way. We hear a lot of people who say that they depend on word of mouth for their marketing. One way to get your customers to market for you is by being worthy of their recommendation. Remember that when a client recommends you, they are putting *their good name* on the line *for you*. There is nothing more embarrassing than to refer someone, only to have your friend tell you about how badly they were treated. And don't forget that people are more apt to tell people about a bad experience than they are a good one. Be worthy.

Huggin' Molly's postcards are simply brilliant in my opinion, but if the service was poor, I wouldn't buy the postcards, much less send them to my friends and family. The postcards are consistent with the theme of the restaurant and demonstrate in a very visual way the nostalgic atmosphere. Interestingly, at least to me, is that the era of the soda shop was one where people were more mannerly, work ethics were higher, traditional values meant something, and service was *very* important. It is not surprising that a business that evokes that kind of aura draws people to it—an oasis of sanity, as it were. But, again, if the customer service did not equal or exceed the expectation of those nostalgic values, we would walk away feeling let down, disappointed, maybe even angry.

What we tell our consulting clients is that there are four very important things that the business owner *has* to do in order to have great customer service:

1) Hire the best people you can
2) Hire people whose personality is suited to the job
3) Train them well, and then have *ongoing, regular* training
4) Have a way to check up on them to make sure that they are doing what you taught them, even when you aren't around

Finally, I want to talk a little bit about the YellaWood banner. As I mentioned before, this is one of the best grassroots marketing techniques that I have *ever* seen. Having a banner on a highly visible, high traffic count area is relatively inexpensive and can result in a pretty good ROI (return on investment). But, having marketing that makes people laugh is like striking gold.

When we laugh or smile, our brains produce all kinds of happy chemicals. That's why smiling and laughing make us feel good. Our brain's reward system is such that it *really* likes this chemistry and will repeat behaviors that create that chemistry. It is addcitive in the sense that we crave that specific chemistry and will do things to recreate it. One of the ways it does that is to recognize what makes us feel happy, and compel us to do it again, and again.

Now, imagine that you could create that kind of reward system in your clients' brains so that every time they think of you, they feel warm and fuzzy. They aren't sure why they feel that way, they just do. They might actually seek you out in order to *be happy,* much like the way you feel when you eat your favorite food from childhood, or a really delicious slice of chocolate cake. You, or your business, become one of their happy places.

The YellaWood banner does that for me. The first time I saw it, I literally laughed out loud. Even now, years later, I smile, not only when I *see* the banner, but when I even *think* about it. When I am in Home Depot getting supplies for one of our home improvement projects, and I see the YellaWood logo on the lumber, I smile! You could struggle for years to try to create that kind of loyalty in your clients' minds, and still not achieve it. But by making me laugh, Jimmy Rane has created a loyal customer.

Photos courtesy of Great Southern Wood Preservation

WireGrassroots Marketing Concepts
Illustrated in This Story

- Have exceptional customer service
- Make them laugh
- Use a large banner on the side of a building in a high traffic area
- Be an interesting destination/experience
- Get your customers to market for you
- Exceed expectations
- Hire great people
- Give people a reason to talk about you in a positive way

Hurst's Wiregrass Taekwondo Center

My daughter is a student at Hurst's Wiregrass Taekwondo Center in Headland. Her involvement with this group over a period of years has given me the opportunity to witness how well Brittany Hurst Jolly and Adam Jolly use grassroots marketing.

It started when Jessica attended a free class and decided to sign up. The program itself is designed to keep the entry level students engaged. There is constant recognition for students' accomplishments. There are goals, and there are measurable steps to the accomplishment of *each* goal.

Beyond how the program is set up to work, though, there are a lot of marketing pieces that are also incorporated in the way that the Jollys run their business. One of the goals that my daughter worked hard for was to be selected for the demo (short for demonstration) team. The demo team competes at tournaments hosted by the American Taekwondo Foundation; and Hurst's Wiregrass Taekwondo Center wins *every* demo team competition that they enter. There is a rigorous try out for the team, even students who have been on the team for years must try out each time. Being part of the team has a lot of bragging rights for the students. They are the best of the best.

The demo team is a big part of the grassroots marketing strategy at this establishment. Beyond the competitions and the huge trophy for being the National Champions, the team also does a lot of public performances. If there is a festival or event in the Headland area, you can bet that the demo team from Hurst's Wiregrass Taekwondo Center will be there.

After the performance, students walk through the audience and hand out the boards that were broken in the performance. The broken boards are then used as coupons for a free class.

Another great grassroots marketing piece that is used by the Jollys is to host Ninja Warrior events. These are evenings held about once a quarter where the students can bring a friend. There is an athletic course laid out inside the facility which includes things like a short zip line, obstacles to overcome, battles with padded 'weapons', etc. There is pizza, and all manner of good things to eat. The kids have fun, Mom and Dad get a night off, and the taekwondo center usually gets new students. There is a fee to attend, so the marketing is self funding (meaning it pays for itself).

You will also see Hurst's Wiregrass Taekwondo Center engaged in various charitable events. One of their higher profile charity events is the annual Cystic Fibrosis Walk. Leading up to the Cystic Fibrosis Walk, students engage in various fund raising activities, such as car washes that are held at the center's facility on Highway 431. All students are encouraged to participate in the walk, but the demo team is *required* to participate. Students (and parents!) buy t-shirts that have the team name on it, with proceeds going to the charity. The demo team performs. As with the demonstrations at festivals and events, the boards that are broken in the performance are handed out as coupons for free classes.

Brittany also runs an after school kids' program at the Hurst's Wiregrass Taekwondo Center. Students must also be enrolled in taekwondo classes in order to attend. The cost for the after school program is very reasonable, and includes set aside time for the kids to eat whatever snacks they might bring, and to do their homework, followed by a kids' taekwondo class.

The after school program allows the Jollys to extend the hours of operation beyond what is normal for this type of business. Working parents whose schedules are already stretched too thin can send their kids to taekwondo lessons, without adding another piece of shrapnel to the hand grenade of overwhelm that they are experiencing. Meanwhile, the parents can feel confident that their kids are supervised after school, they will get their homework done, and they will *actually* get some exercise.

There are so many things that the folks at Hurst's Wiregrass Taekwondo Center are doing right; it should be a model that other business owners study.

How *You* Can Use It

Customer engagement is another topic that is often in the headlines these days. When your customers aren't engaged, they forget about you. The challenge becomes, how can you create something that keeps *you* in their 'top of mind consciousness'? How do you stay relevant to them on an ongoing, frequent basis? How do you keep them from forgetting about you?

In this crazy, attention deficit world that we live in, it is imperative that your clients don't get bored with you. For some businesses, customer engagement is relatively easy. For others it might be more of a challenge. I'll let you in on a little secret I learned, if you promise not to tell anyone! The best way to keep to keep your clients interested in what you are doing, is to be interested in what *they* are doing, and to be relevant to that. *Shhhhhh!* Remember, it's our little secret!

Interestingly, there is an unspoken social contract that pretty much requires that if someone is interested in what you are doing, you must reciprocate by being interested in what *they* are doing. Further, people in general are starved for recognition and appreciation, and anyone who can give them that is *more valuable than all the treasures throughout the world.* It is a priceless commodity because it is so rare.

Beyond being interested in what they are doing, and giving them recognition and appreciation (which Hurst's Wiregrass Taekwondo does in spades, by the way!), you also need to have a lot of variety, so things don't get stale. *Always* be up to something, beyond business as usual. Give them something to talk about. When you give them something interesting to talk about, guess what, they are marketing for you!

Believe it or not, there are a 'bragging rights' in being associated with someone who is the best at what they do. It's part of our confirmation bias that if we associate with people who are highly successful, some of that success rubs off on us, because we ch*oose* to be part of their world. We are smart for selecting the best, therefore, we are also the best.

Even if you can't be the National Champion like the demo team at Hurst's Wiregrass Taekwondo Center, you can still become a recognized authority on a topic. I have seen people who weren't necessarily the best at what they did, but they were able to do something like writing an article for the newspaper. Others had a friend record them on video while they repaired something, and discussed each step as they did it. They posted their video on YouTube, and *voila!* they became a recognized authority on the topic. Still others attended a special class that wasn't available in the local area and became certified on a topic. You don't have to be an authority on *everything* that you do, but *you can find **one** thing*, and become an expert on that.

Being involved in charity work is a great way to show your client base that you are part of the community, and that you are following the Bible's edict of being of service to your fellow man. This is an area where the local business owner can really shine. After all, you aren't some big corporate entity. You are a local. You live here. You care about the people. *You are one of us.*

The charity can be something that is close to your heart, or it can be a charity that is significant to your community. For example, we live in a community with a strong agricultural base. There are a lot of problems with the bees, our natural pollinators, dying off. Without pollination, the crops won't fruit. No fruiting, no peanuts, cotton or tomatoes to harvest. No harvest, or reduced harvest means that farming businesses can't survive. Becoming involved with a charity that focuses on educating the public about how certain pesticides are contributing to the collapse of bee colonies *might* be pretty significant to the Wiregrass.

We also have a strong military base in our area, and with that, a lot of military vets. If you are a veteran and own a business, you are working from a position of strength, and that fact could be used quite effectively in your marketing. But, you don't have to be a vet in order to contribute to our military and military veteran community. You could hire vets. You could contribute a portion of sales to help take care of our disabled vets. You could give discounts to the veterans in the area.

It may sound like I am being somewhat cynical about using charity work for marketing purposes. But you, as a community member, really *do* understand the importance of being a good steward in order to help the people where you live. You know that there are people who are less fortunate than you are, and that it is your responsibility to do what you can to help them. We *must* be part of something larger than ourselves. If every person and part of your home town is not being supported with their struggles in some way, they cannot have a better life, and the overall health of your hometown will suffer as a result.

Finally, let's look at how expanding your services from what you are already doing can make you more valuable to your client base. For the Jollys, adding the after school program does something valuable for the parents of the students, as well as helping the Jollys to expand the normal business hours of their industry. It's a win-win situation. All of the extra activities like the parents' night out, provides extra services that are valuable to the parents. Requiring that students maintain good grades in order to participate, helps the parents. The extra value that Hurst's Wiregrass Taekwondo Center provides makes the cost, both in money and in the very real expense of time, much more valuable than the simple exchange of money for classes.

Another example of a local company that has found a way to expand valuable services is a local air conditioning repair company. They offer a subscription service. The service provides two valuable things to the customer. First, it provides a check up and service prior to peak air conditioning season so that your system doesn't fail during the hot Alabama summers. Second, in the event that you *do* have an equipment issue during peak season, subscription members get priority in the service line up. What does the business get from the subscription service? They keep their staff busy during slow periods so that they have adequate service providers during the summer to handle the high demand, *and* it helps to pay for that staffing requirement year round.

Yet another example: most of the corporate chains of auto service have a version of the free 15 point checkup. The customer is assured that they can take that family vacation without fearing a break down…as much. The auto service center gets the opportunity to look for additional services while they are doing the job that they were hired to do. The additional service, can be scheduled at a future date, if it isn't pressing, which helps them to fill the pipeline for next week or next month.

Two years ago I had a water treatment system installed at the house. The installation tech noticed that I did not have a faucet on that side of the house. A problem that I had complained about for years, by the way. He offered to put one in while he was installing the system…at no charge. Heck, yeah! The other day, the faucet sprang a leak. I tried to repair it myself, because that's the way I was raised. However, when Dad was teaching me how to do basic household repairs, they didn't have Nynex, and I had no clue of how the coupling and the Nynex were connected. Eventually, I gave up and called the water treatment system company, even though the problem was not with their system, but with the free add on service they provided. Within a couple of days, the tech who installed the faucet came out, and within 15 minutes, he had repaired it. Talk about service above and beyond!

Regardless of your industry, there is *something* that you can do to add value to your customers, and often you can charge extra for it.

WireGrassroots Marketing Concepts Illustrated in This Story

- Keep your customers engaged in what you are doing

- Get your customers to do your marketing

- Be the best at what you do

- Give your clients something to talk about/brag about

- Become a recognized authority on the topic

- Get involved with a charity

- Add additional services to what you are already doing that fills a need that your clients have

Ravenwood Sporting Clays

OK, I admit it, I have a particular interest in gun clubs. I love shooting. Whether it is a pistol match, or just 'plinking' lead down range to improve my speed and accuracy, there is something very liberating and energizing in having the skill to control a dangerous weapon.

Even though I don't shoot long guns, I like to visit Ravenwood. This particular facility has a jaw dropping *"WOW! Factor"*. After visiting Ravenwood, you can't **help** but tell people about it. When you arrive and enter the clubhouse, your attention is immediately drawn to the indoor fire pit. There is no question that you are in an exclusive club or hunting lodge.

You are greeted by a friendly and knowledgeable staff person and the facility's dog-in-residence, who will probably bring you his stuffed squirrel to play fetch with. If you have never visited the club before, you will probably be offered a tour or the use of a golf cart, so that you can discover the many interesting shooting stages that comprise the course. Each stage has a covered shooting house that is well constructed and *immaculately* maintained. As you drive your golf cart through the meandering wooded paths throughout the 43 acre grounds, you might spy a Sasquatch walking through the woods near one of the stages. It's a little bit of whimsy that I've been told is moved around the property from time to time. You never know where you will spot Bigfoot, seemingly ambling through the grounds.

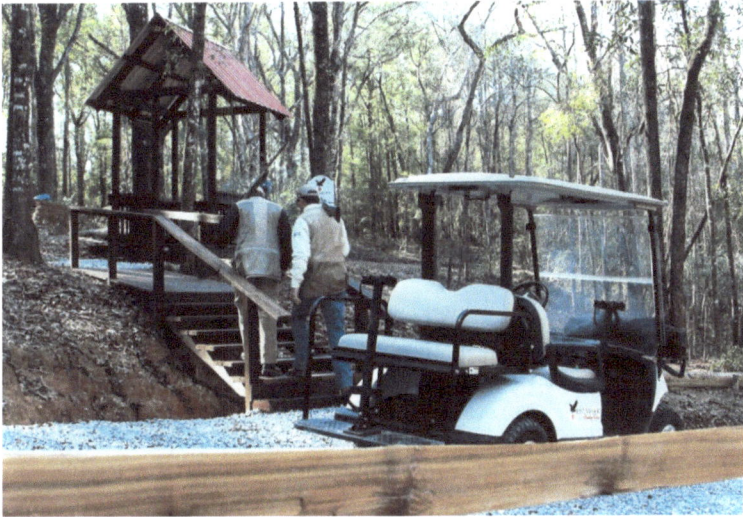

Like many of the grassroots marketers in this area, Ravenwood also hosts events (many of which are sponsored by vendors who sell shooting supplies and equipment). At the last sporting clays match that I attended at Ravenwood, the atmosphere reminded me of a plantation era weekend hunting party. There were rocking chairs on the back porch where those who weren't shooting were mingling, sipping ice cold drinks, and playing fetch with the dog. All that was missing to complete the scene were fine cigars and brandy.

I was also impressed to see Ravenwood co-sponsoring an event at the National Peanut Festival grounds a while back. They had an elevated covered wooden structure (like one of the stages on their course) where people could climb up and get a better view of what was going on around the performance stage. There was a large banner stretched across the platform with their name. Talk about a visible presence!

I've received marketing from Ravenwood announcing that a professional shooter was coming to the facility and offering classes, and instruction. The *Expert From Afar* is always a great tool to bring in people who are both willing, and able, to spend money on the things that are important to them.

How <u>You</u> Can Use It

"Wow! Factor" is a huge part of getting clients to market for you, whether it is in the layout of your facility, or over the top customer service. Anytime you can get people to spontaneously say, **"Wow!"** you've achieved creating a positive, and noteworthy image of your business in their minds.

Think of Disney for a moment. No matter how often you go to Disney World, it's impressive. For one thing, it's massive. Then it is clean…always. No matter how many thousands of people have been through those gates on any given day, you won't find trash and clutter. Every single person who works there is doing what they should be doing, when they are supposed to be doing it. None of the staff are 'winging it'. They are scripted, and they practice that script until they probably mumble it in their sleep. You won't find a Disney staff member who has a problem with what they are doing, no matter how they might feel on any given day.

With my background and training, I can be pretty critical, *especially* of businesses, so when an establishment can make *me* say, *"Wow!"*, it's something. People who don't know that I am a business consultant, might not 'get' that when I talk about how great a place is, it means that *I couldn't find anything that I would change*. They wowed me. Such it is with Ravenwood.

The first time I drove through those massive black iron gates, I said, *"Wow!"* Then, when I walked into the clubhouse, I said, "Holy (explicative)". J.D. has created a gentleman's hunting club, right here in rural Alabama. There is *nothing* like it in the greater Dothan area. If you want to see what a true *Wow!* looks like, I strongly suggest that you tour Ravenwood.

While not every business can afford to create such an awe inspiring facility, pretty much *every* business can create a *"Wow! Factor"* with their service. Just the other day we were at lunch at a local sandwich shop. I have come to expect that most of these places have absentee owners and poorly trained, underpaid staff. I don't expect much, and I usually get less than that.

Imagine my surprise when the owner came out from behind the counter and said, "Thank you for spending your money here. I know you could have gone anywhere else in town for lunch, but you *chose* to come here and spend your money with me. I appreciate that." *Wow!* I rarely hear anyone say, "thank you", much less such an effusive appreciation of my patronage. I talked about it for at least an hour, till Larry was sick of hearing it.

"Wow! Factor" can come in many forms, and one of those forms is in exceeding customer expectations. The facility at Ravenwood is impressive, but the staff also creates a *Wow!* by being so well trained, courteous, and knowledgeable. I am not a client. As I mentioned before, I don't do well with long guns. Yet, even though I am not a potential member, every time I have visited the facility, I was treated as if I were a valued client. They don't blow me off because I'm not part of their sport. They treat me like a guest at their hunting lodge. More than willing to make me comfortable at the lodge house, or set me up with a golf cart so I can ride around and enjoy the gorgeous setting, while looking for that hidden Sasquatch.

Savvy grassroots marketers find ways to create *Wow!* Sometimes it is the little things that are memorable. My husband and business partner was a chiropractor for over thirty years. I was in the office one day when one of his patients came in holding a piece of paper in his hand. It was a letter that Larry had sent him after the patient's first visit…over 20 years before. That simple letter so impressed the patient, that he kept the letter for all those years. And he brought it in for Larry to see that *he still had the letter*. It didn't take a lot of effort for Larry to write the letter, but the impact that it had was ***massive***.

No matter what your business is, no matter the industry, no matter what your budget looks like, there is *something* that you can do to create a *"Wow! Factor"*.

The *"Expert from Afar"* is another interesting concept of Grassroots Marketing. We're all familiar with the old saying, "Familiarity breeds contempt", and there is a lot of truth in that. We tend to take people we know for granted. We give them less credit for what they know because we know their shortcomings, and for some reason, those shortcomings bleed over to color their strengths as well. An *"Expert from Afar"* can teach you something that someone you know can't, simply because you are more liable to listen to them and believe what they say. People will pay a lot of money for an *"Expert from Afar"* to teach them something. They will come out to attend a session with the *"Expert from Afar"*, because it is a one day only event. Interestingly, bringing in an *"Expert from Afar"* creates more credibility for the person who hosts the session. I guess being smart enough to host the *"Expert from Afar"* and being able to persuade that expert to come to your facility makes us more credible as well.

Getting sponsors for your events works in a similar way. The fact that sponsors are willing to have their name associated with your business give you automatic credibility. Not only can you get instant credibility from these sponsors, they can also help you fund the event or the marketing for it. The sponsoring might be cash to help fund the marketing or cost of the event, or it might be some sort of in kind service. For example, the guy that owns a sign company might co-op the event with you by providing signs in exchange for his business being promoted on the signs as well. A plant nursery might provide plants as a backdrop for a fundraiser with a discreet sign that lets people know that they provided the plants.

Ravenwood uses sponsors in multiple ways, including discounts on ammunition for their matches. And, by the same token, Ravenwood also helps sponsor other events. This, to me, is what networking is all about. This is the true power of networking…business owners working together for each other's benefit, and everyone involved gets something out of the relationship.

Photos courtesy of Ravenwood Sporting Clays

**WireGrassroots Marketing Concepts
Illustrated in This Story**

- Have a *"WOW! Factor"*
- Exceed customer expectations for friendliness and service
- Be the best at what you do
- Give people something to talk about/brag about
- Sponsor community events
- Get sponsors for the events that you host
- Bring in an *Expert From Afar*

Friend Bank

One of the advantages to being a locally owned company is the ability to be part of the community in ways that corporate organizations can't. Locals may work for or manage a local branch office, but they don't really have any authority. Home Office dictates what will be done, and when it will be done. The local office or branch has little, if any, say in process or procedure. Additionally, turnover can be pretty high in these organizations, so today's manager is likely to be replaced within a couple of years.

On the other hand, consumers *know* the owner of a local business. They recognize that a local is more accountable to the community than a huge corporate entity, where you can't talk to anyone who is ultimately responsible. This gives the local business owner an advantage, but it also requires that you behave in a way that is above reproach. If you are going to be sitting in church in front of your customers, you had better make sure that you are treating them right! And your customers *know* that. Even if the consumer doesn't know you personally, they feel like they do, and that approachability is the local business owner's secret weapon.

Hope Johnson of Friend Bank knows this lesson of grassroots marketing quite well. Friend exemplifies this aspect of grassroots marketing in such a way, that they *own* it.

Recently, I have been getting a lot of updates from them about how they are teaching financial principals to area grade school students. Most of the materials for the classes are provided by the FDIC. All Friend has to do is to order the supplies from the FDIC, set up the classes with the schools, and send a knowledgeable staff member who can work with young kids to teach the classes. Friend is 'raising' their own future clients, by being very involved in educating kids on a topic that most *adults* struggle with.

Friend also 'strongly encourages' staff members to get involved with local charity groups or service groups. Before Friend switched from hard copy newsletter to digital social media for staying in touch with customers, every issue had at least one article about staff members volunteering in the community. Staff members work with whatever service group they have an affinity for, provided it is reputable and not surrounded by negatively controversial topics. They are a very visible presence in the community, and that reinforces Friend's message, "We are part of *this* community."

What better way to tell the community that you are part of it, and that you support helping others and being of service, than to have a meeting room that can be used for service organization or community improvement group meetings? It's pretty brilliant, really. The bank needs the meeting room for staff meetings and board meetings, but the room is only used as needed, and sits idle most of the time. Friend has taken occasional use space and made it available to the community, without increasing their overhead at all.

When Friend Bank first rebranded themselves as Friend (formerly Slocomb National Bank), they also brought in a mascot--a miniature dachshund named Buddy. Buddy runs to greet you when you walk in the door. He is small enough that he is not threatening in any way. You can't help but smile when the little guy runs up to you, wags his tail, and looks at you adoringly with those puppy dog eyes. More importantly, I think, is that people who might not normally come inside the bank, preferring online banking or the drive through, will come in to visit Buddy. This face to face interaction allows staff to be able to build better *personal* relationships with customers.

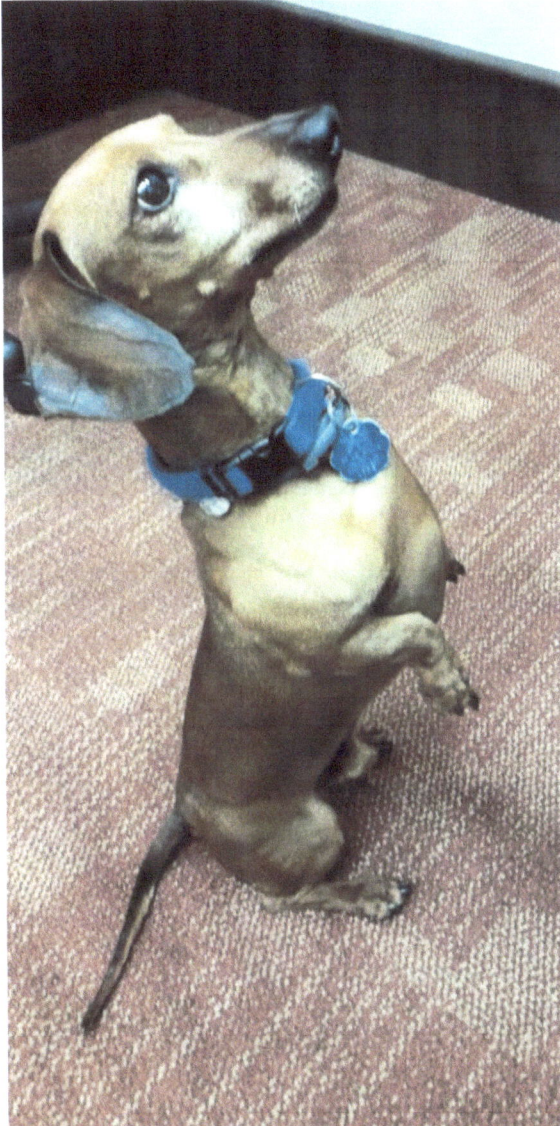

Something else that Hope did when she rebranded Slocomb National Bank as Friend bank came when the Dothan branch was being constructed. For years, there had been an elderly man who sold boiled peanuts at that location. And, while many in the community were happy to see the seedy, derelict, run down, abandoned gas station on that site being torn down, quite a few lamented that the Peanut Man might lose his spot.

What most did not realize at the time, was that provisions were being made, not only for the Peanut Man to continue to do business at the location, but to build a structure on the property where he would be protected from the weather.

Unfortunately, the Peanut Man passed away before construction was completed. Did Friend Bank abandon its plans for the Peanut Man's shelter? Of course not! He was a local icon. The gazebo was built a park bench was added. One of the iconic Peanuts About Town statues was erected in the Peanut Man's honor, along with a plaque that tells his story.

Being part of the local community and demonstrating their responsibility to the community earns Friend Bank a wag of the tail in my WireGrassroots Marketing Hall of Fame.

How <u>You</u> Can Use It

In the interest of full disclosure, I should mention here that I have a lot of family ties to Friend Bank. It has been in my family for three generations, and I might be a little biased on their behalf.

Even though I have never worked in the bank, I've been privy to some of the inner workings of the bank. Sometimes through conversations about what was going on, or what plans were being made, sometimes through stories of the past.

Trust is an imperative in any business, but in a business where you are entrusted with the safety of people's money, trust is even more important.

One of my favorite stories revolves around the Great Depression. This was a time when banks were failing, and people were afraid they would lose all their money if their bank went under. The story goes something like this. Granddaddy, understanding that banking, in general, had lost its trust with the client base, decided that the only way to assure his depositors that their money was safe, and avoid a run on the bank (which surely would have shut it down), was to create an over the top demonstration to his customers that they needn't worry.

He ordered enough cash from the Fed to cover every single deposit. He took these stacks of cash, put them in crab traps, and stacked them on the counter behind the teller's cages. When customers came in to withdraw their money, they saw stacks and stacks of cold hard cash, which assured them that the bank was solvent. Granddaddy was prepared to give them their cash, if they felt they couldn't trust the bank. However, the story is that upon seeing the stacks of cash, not a single depositor closed their account.

No matter what your business or industry, building and maintaining trust is vital. The easiest way to do that is to have a policy of doing what you say you will do, when you say you will do it. The second easiest way to build trust is by offering a strong guarantee.

There are other stories about how my grandfather often bought homes that were for sale. Some of these homes were then 'rented' to widows and women who had been 'abandoned' by their husbands. The rent was often discounted, or in extreme circumstances, no rent was charged. He also worked with his brothers, who owned a local store, to provide groceries to these families where there was no father.

Throughout the generations that have owned the bank, there has always been a strong sense of responsibility to the community. One way that was reflected was in the establishment of a trust that provided Christmas dinner to the less fortunate. Other ways included the establishment of scholarships for young students from Slocomb, where the bank started, and the creation of the first senior citizen center in the state, which are now in almost every town throughout Alabama.

The president and CEO has *always* had an understanding of the importance of being of service that goes beyond the normal tenets of being a business owner. The bank is not just a bank, it is a foundation for the success of the community, and it (and its leaders and staff) work hard at fulfilling that position.

You probably are not in the position of being able to fund scholarships or set up trust funds to feed people on Christmas, but you can still be a part of this type of vision. Last year, we went down to see if we could help with the Turkeys from Heaven project in Dothan.

The pavilion at the Peanut Festival grounds was full of business owners (and/or their staff) laboring over smokers, where turkeys were being cooked. Over 2,200 meals were provided to Dothan families for Christmas dinner. Not everyone was cooking, some were loading the cooked turkeys, others were unloading raw turkeys to be cooked, and still others were packaging the meals, or picking up donations of side dishes. On the final day, people were using their own vehicles to deliver the meals.

I do not have any financial interest in the bank, and am rarely privy to its inner workings anymore, but under the leadership of the generations of Harrises, I have watched the bank grow and expand. Even in the recent recession, where many banks were failing, and trust in banks was low, Friend continued to be healthy and to expand. They hold one of the highest bank ratings of all thr banks in the area, and I truly believe that is due to the way that the bank's stewardship and the community stewardship has been interwoven throughout its history.

No matter what the size of your own organization may be, you can be a force of good in some way. Whether it is a donation of cash, an in kind donation, or providing your staff with ways to be of service, like educating the public on a topic that you are an expert on, you can make a difference. Sometimes, just being kind and offering people a smile can have a huge effect. People remember kindness and friendliness, especially in the environment that we now find ourselves.

If you can make these things part of the foundation of your business, your customers will respond positively.

Photos courtesy of Friend Bank

**WireGrassroots Marketing Concepts
Illustrated in This Story**

- *BE* part of the community
- Greet customers with enthusiasm
- Be of service to the community
- Make occasional use space available for service organizations
- Encourage staff to be of service to the community
- 'Raise' your own future clients
- Be a trusted authority by providing free education on your industry topic
- Respect and pay homage to community icons

Folklore Brewery and Meadery

Gotta hand it to Jeremy Pate of Folklore Brewery and Meadery. He does a *lot* of grassroots marketing.

One of the grassroots marketing techniques that we have not covered is that of cooperative marketing. Step inside Folklore's taproom, and you will see cooperative marketing on almost every wall. Huge banners emblazoned with the name and logo of almost every restaurant that Jeremy supplies beer to line the walls. Since the taproom has limited hours that it is open to the public, this allows patrons to know where they can get an ice cold Grateful Red IPA any day of the week.

Rather than trying to run the brewery and taproom, as well as providing food (always a good idea when you sell alcohol), Jeremy co-ops with food vendors for on premises consumption. In the early days, these were food trucks, but in the last year or so, Fly By Night catering has opened an onsite food service in a separate section of Folklore's building. This allows Jeremy to concentrate on what he does best…make beer and mead.

Jeremy also distinguishes his brewery by creating an atmosphere of camaraderie. Folklore likens it to "having a beer in a buddy's backyard" and further promotes the neighborly environment with their motto, "*It's the beer that binds us.*" There are any number of sports bars in the area, where people gather to watch a game and drink a beer. Instead of customers being glued to a TV set and ignoring the people around them, Folklore customers are hanging out in the yard by a fire pit (in the cooler months) and playing games such as Giant Jenga, Cards Against Humanity, and Cornhole. The convivial atmosphere encourages people to talk to others whom they don't know very well (or at all). Socially friendly dogs are welcome to come, too, and hang out.

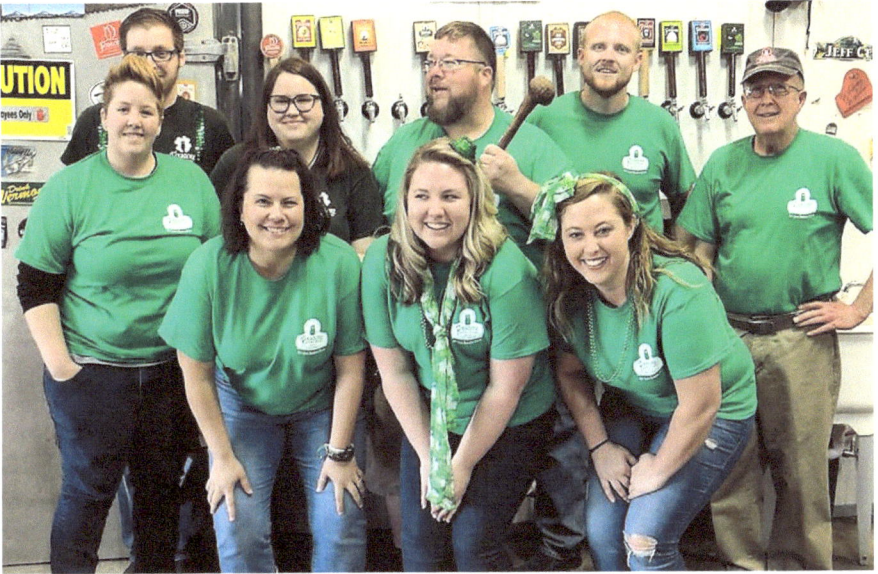

Folklore does a lot of benefit promotions and three of their favorite charities are military veterans, animal rescue groups, and simply taking care of their fellow man. During the Hurricane Irma evacuation, the area was full of people who came here to get out of harm's way. People were in a frenzy to stock up on water, and stores were selling out at an incredible rate. And then I saw a Facebook post from Folklore that they had pallets of water available for *anyone* who needed it. No charge. Take what you need.

There are a lot of craft breweries around these days, and I would be remiss if I didn't mention how Jeremy has distinguished himself in his industry. Folklore is the *only* brewery I have encountered that also makes mead. Mead is made from honeyed water that is fermented in yeast. It has a slightly sweet flavor, without being overly sweet. While mead isn't that popular in America, it does have its own following, and just having it on the menu provides Folklore with a way to make themselves a *category of one* in the growing craft brewery industry.

I also love the way Folklore pays tribute to the area by naming their brews after Southern traditions. There is Snipe Hunt IPA,

Wiregrass Wheat, Front Porch Pale Ale, and Cotton Tale Pale Ale. There are also the beers that are named in honor of Fort Rucker:JP-8, Shadowcaster Porter, and Golden Hawk Kolsch. Paying homage to the past is an integral part of being part of the local community, and it is one that most corporate businesses from outside of the area either don't get, or can't do well simply because the policy makers just aren't from around here.

Customer service is one of the most important weapons in the grassroots marketers' arsenal, and Folklore does this extremely well. Sit outside on the porch to enjoy your beer, and it won't be long before a staff member stops by to make sure you have everything you need. And, that lady in the electric scooter who stops to visit at every table, and offer a taste of the newest creation? That is Jerrilyn, who prefers to be called Mom.

How <u>You</u> Can Use It

Folklore has managed to position themselves as a category of one. They are the *only* craft brewery in town. They are also the *only* craft brewery in the area that makes mead. As discussed previously, every business **must** find a way to present themselves in a way that the competition does not. Face it, you can only lower your prices so far and stay in business. Cutting prices is not a strategy that you can afford to pursue. There have been many instances of businesses with deep pockets that have a strategy of selling at below cost in order to force out competition. It's a battle that you can't win. However, once you have established your own Unique Selling Proposition, you can not only get more customers, you will get customers who are willing to pay more.

The Wiregrass has very deep, traditional roots. Our history and our traditions are sacred to us. God, family, country, high school football games, college rivalries, peanuts and cotton, our boys (and girls) in uniform, sitting on the porch, chasing fireflies. Traditions that are held near and dear to our hearts. These things define us. They define us as individuals, as groups, and as business owners. The more you can pay homage to these roots, the more your customers who share these values will relate to your business.

Photos courtesy of Folklore Brewery and Meadery

**WireGrassroots Marketing Concepts
Illustrated in This Story**

- Co-op with complementary businesses
- Exceed customer expectations for friendliness and service
- Find a way to make yourself a category of one
- Acknowledge and provide for those things that are important to your clients
- Host benefit events

Earnie's Snowballs

Speaking of co-operative marketing, I'd be remiss if I didn't mention Earnie's Snowballs. Let me tell you a little bit about how we met Earnie.

A few years ago, Larry and I decided to join the Dothan Area Young Professionals. We kept hearing all this stuff in the media about how bad the Millennials were, we thought we would check it out and see if they really *were* as bad as people were saying they were. Well, the media was wrong! We found all kinds of interesting people at the DAYP, including Earnie.

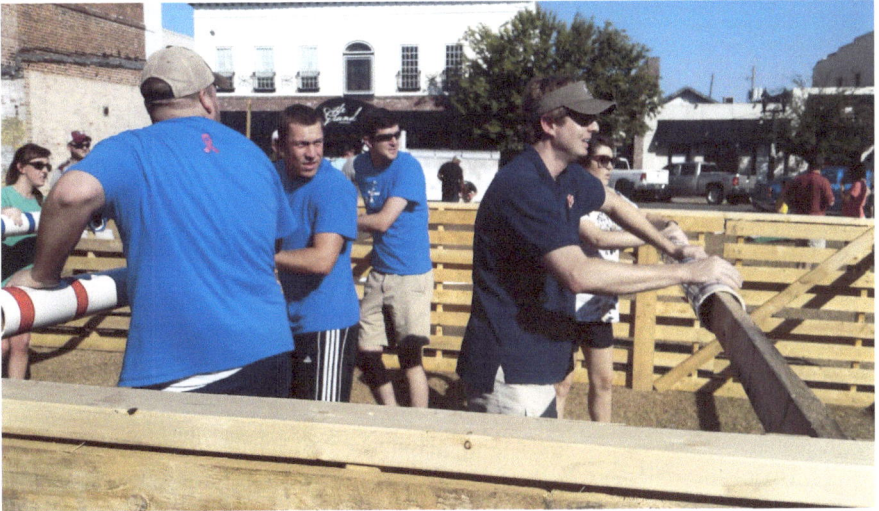

The first time we saw Earnie was at the Human Foosball Tournament that the DAYP was sponsoring. This is a fund-raising event where the foosball table is people sized. Human beings line up to be the goalies, defenders and attackers. A soccer ball is kicked around and you try and score on the other human team. Earnie had a food truck there. The snowballs were quite refreshing after such a heated competition.

The next time that we ran into Earnie, was at the Thirsty Pig. We saw a post on the DAYP Facebook page that they were having a chili dog contest at the Thirsty Pig. Since the Thirsty Pig had just opened and we'd never been there, we thought we'd give it a try. When we got there, they had 3 chili dog vendors competing for this event. Earnie was the only local. Now, one of the things that Grassroots Marketers do is, they find a way to position themselves so that they can win. When you've got 3 contestants, and only one of them is local, guess who's going to win? You got it, the local guy!

One of the things that we discovered when we were at that contest was that Earnie was highly conversant and energetic. This guy is a dynamo! He was just *so excited* about what he was doing. He couldn't wait to tell you about his grandmother's chili dog recipe, and how everybody loves it, and the people who work for him just love their job because they love the product. This guy is dynamic.

After talking to Earnie a little bit, we found out something else about him that is somewhat unusual. He actually *buys* books about business--and he doesn't just buy books, he *reads* them, I mean, how crazy is that?

Something else Earnie does that's really great is that like Folklore, Earnie's has a Unique Selling Proposition. His USP is his grandmother's recipe, which is different from any chili dog I've ever tasted. It's very distinctive. It's not "open a can of Castleberry's and spread it on your chili dog". It's *Grandma's recipe* and it's unique.

Earnie also has a mission that's very important to him. You see, Earnie has had a difficult past in that he has had jobs that were suddenly cancelled. It wasn't that he was fired or laid off, it's that the company shut down and suddenly he had no income. So, his mission is not only to provide jobs but to provide *stable* employment for locals. I think that a very important aspect of being part of a community is to recognize that the people you hire are dependent upon you for their income.

Getting back to co-operative marketing, Earnie does that in a couple of different ways. One of them is that during crawfish season, he allows Cajun Roots Crawfish to set up in conjunction with his standing structure; he provides them with a refrigerated unit to keep the crawfish from spoiling in the heat. He lets them put out signs in front of his business. He posts blasts about it on his Facebook page. Earnie is helping to support another business that's temporary and has no standing structure. I've also seen co-operative marketing being used by Earnie for Foster Fest. He sets up inside The Grand and at another outside location. So, while he's marketing himself, by mentioning where he is located at the event, he's also marketing The Grand.

In addition to the standing location in the parking lot of the Circle West, Earnie's also goes to where his clients are; he has two food trucks and those food trucks go to events where people are gathering. Anywhere that it's hot and sticky, and it's Alabama, and it's the middle of summer--and wouldn't a snow cone be just perfect?

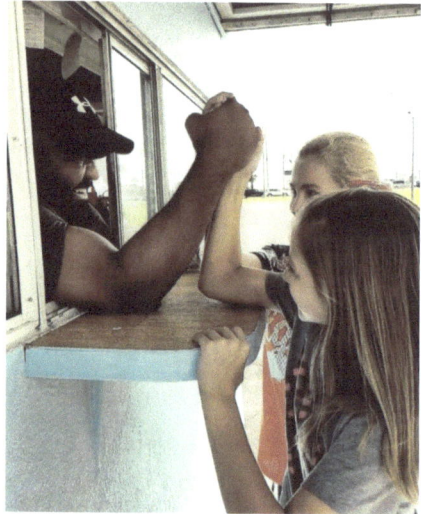

Lately, I've seen Earnie incorporating another wonderful Grassroots Marketing concept which is using contests. You've got to love the uniqueness of one of his promotions which is "Arm Wrestle Earnie for a Snowcone". Now, this guy has some guns on him, he's got biceps that you might see on somebody who's in the military and works out all the time. I mean, his arms are huge and he's got these kids arm wrestling him for a free snowball.

Finally, I'd like to talk about how much Earnie is out and about now. I mentioned that he was at the Human Foosball Tournament and the Thirsty Pig. He also was at an event at Harley Davidson of Dothan. He's at the Screen on the Green at the Wiregrass Museum of Art. You can't go anywhere that there's something happening in the Wiregrass without running into Earnie.

How <u>You</u> Can Use It

Let's look at how we could take some of the lessons that we've seen being used by Earnie's Snowballs, and incorporate them into your business. We've mentioned co-operative marketing a couple of times and, you know, I've been pretty basic about that. The simplest model is that I put up a sign in my place for your business, you put up a sign in your place for my business and that is co-operative marketing. However, there are ways you can expand that.

One of the big things in marketing these days is called Event Marketing. Event Marketing is where you create an event that people come to and they're exposed to your business as a result. Well, there are a lot of things that might be required to have an event, you might need signs-- if nothing else just directing people to where they should go. And there are businesses in this area that are sign companies. It's what they do. You might work out a trade where the signs have a small print on them that reads, *"Courtesy of XYZ Signs".* That gets their marketing in front of people. This is especially true if the event is some sort of fund raiser or community service project.

Another situation might be one where if you have a speaker standing at a podium, you might want to have some potted plants around the podium to kind of dress it up and make it look less stark. There are nurseries in the area that sell potted plants. They might be persuaded to loan you some plants in exchange for the co-operative marketing or they might give you a discount for it. Again, you have a sign, *"These plants courtesy of XYZ Nursery".*

You might need food vendors for your event. Again, co-operative marketing. Your event might need bounce houses for the kids and or food trucks like Earnie's. These vendors would market that they're going to be at your event, and that would bring people who normally go to these businesses, but wouldn't necessarily go to yours.

We also talked a lot about having a Unique Selling Proposition. One of the consultants that I like to talk to asks, "Why, out of all the options available to them, should they use you?" There are too many Chinese food and Barbecue restaraunts in the Dothan area to count. Why should they go to your Chinese place rather than someone else's? Why should they go to your barbecue place rather than someone else's? Well, you could have a special recipe with secret ingredients that nobody else has, or you could have a buffet that has so many choices that it has a *"Wow! Factor".*

I can't say enough about how important customer service is, and that is a great way to distinguish yourself from other people. Customer service is so bad, these days that just having staff members who can *actually service a customer* can make you stand out from the crowd. Whatever it is that you do, find yourself a Unique Selling Proposition and distinguish yourself from the crowd. In some cases, having a great guarantee could be a USP. If you can guarantee people that you will give them *all* of their money back, no questions asked, that's a Unique Selling Proposition because most businesses make you jump through so many hoops to get a refund that it isn't worth it. If you don't already have a USP, you need to find a way to create one.

I mentioned Earnie's enthusiasm, and boy is that *contagious*. Whenever you talk to Earnie, he's excited. Sometimes we get so buried in the day to day minutiae of our jobs that we lose the enthusiasm, we lose the excitement. We have to find a way to create excitement, for ourselves, as well as for our customers. One thing that helps create excitement is adding a new product, I mean, not just any product--but a product that *you're* excited about. As I mentioned before, event marketing is very hot right now. Having an event creates excitement, there's just no way around it. I mean, you've got all kinds of new stuff going on. You've got the build-up. You've got the marketing for it. You're going to have food. You're going to have music. You're going to have bounce houses. And everybody's going to come out have fun. That's exciting! Anything you can do that creates new interest, enthusiasm, and excitement for yourself, for your staff, and for your clients. Let's get excited! Let's get happy!

How can you apply studying and learning new things and incorporating them into your business? Well, most people have a pretty set standard business model and they *might* read their industry's journals and publication. They *might* even read books about what their industry is doing. They *might* read newsletters. They rarely step out of their industry. And when that happens, you kind of get stuck in your thinking.

I'm always reading new things, and one of the authors that I read regularly suggests reading autobiographies of successful people. One of the books that I read was a book by the Mayflower Madam, Sydney Biddle Barrows. Now, I don't own a Cat House. I have no intention of opening a brothel, but reading this book showed me a lot about how marketing—all marketing—uses fantasy. And talk about over-the-top customer service! The book really expanded my thinking on those topics.

WireGrassroots Marketing

Stepping outside of your industry and exposing yourself to what other people are doing and what's being done successfully, and then looking at how you can find parallels for whatever business you're in, will expand your consciousness and it'll make it easy for you to be able to *do new things which will create excitement and enthusiasm.*

Photos courtesy of Earnie's Snowballs

WireGrassroots Marketing Concepts
Illustrated in This Story

- **In a head-to-head competition, set yourself up to win**
- **Use cooperative marketing and space with complementary businesses**
- **Be enthusiastic**
- **Study, and apply, what is known to work**

Closing Thoughts

Once upon a time, there were small stores in every community. The proprietor knew his customers, and they knew him. He didn't need to run ads for customers to know about his business. But, he *did* market.

He went to church, town meetings, and socials. He shared the same concerns as the townspeople. He knew what they needed, and he provided it. He understood that he was an important part of his community. He also knew that his very livelihood depended on his customers thinking well of him and his business, because there were *no new* customers to woo. He had to earn the loyalty of his clients every day, with every transaction.

With the explosion of buying that was created during the heyday of the baby boomer generation, merchants forgot some of the basics of marketing. We got lazy, till the economy collapsed in 2008.As a result of this evolution, most marketing has been simply become a price war, resulting in ever slimmer profit margins. We have trained consumers to wait for a better deal.

In his seminal work, **Spending Waves**, demographic economist Harry S. Dent proves that the reduced birthrate following the baby boomer generation translates into fewer consumers for the next few years. As with our historic merchants of yesteryear, we also have no new consumers to woo. We have too many businesses offering the same merchandise or services, and competition for consumer dollars is desperate. Merchants are slashing prices in order to stay afloat, and the number of empty commercial properties is staggering..

The good news is that when you look at the birth rate charts, you will see an echo boom that is even larger than the baby boom. Additionally, this echo boom is poised to inherit trillions of dollars in the coming years. ***This will be the largest wealth transfer in the history of the world.***

WireGrassroots Marketing

Now is the time for the small, locally owned business to step up to the plate and prove what most of us already knew—local business is here to stay, and we are part of the community. Now is the time to establish relationships with the coming explosion of soon-to-be-wealthy consumers. Grassroots marketing is the sweet spot for doing that. But, as I've said repeatedly throughout this book, if your customer service or your ability to meet and exceed customers' requirements aren't adequate, then effective marketing will only speed up your demise. We have a bit of a sweet spot right now—a period to hone our marketing skills and improve our facilities, the ability to handle customers, and to sharpen our administrations. Once that echo boom of Millennials hits their stride and inherit their parents' wealth, we had better be prepared to *Wow!* them with our ability to be *the* choice for their loyal business, or we will lose the opportunity forever.

C'mon WireGrassroots Marketing Warriors, let's roll!

WireGrassroots Marketing

www.ingramcontent.com/pod-product-compliance
Lightning Source LLC
Chambersburg PA
CBHW041715200326
41519CB00001B/172